best friends

best friends

witty meaningful quotes on friendship

edited by anne howard

Published in North America in 2006
by Tangent Publications
an imprint of
Axis Publishing Limited
8c Accommodation Road
London NW11 8ED
www.axispublishing.co.uk

Creative Director: Siân Keogh
Editorial Director: Anne Yelland
Production Manager: Jo Ryan

ISBN 1-904707-27-0

2 4 6 8 10 9 7 5 3 1

Printed and bound in China

about this book

Best Friends brings together an inspirational selection of powerful, life-affirming, and humorous phrases about friendship and combines them with evocative and gently amusing animal photographs that bring out the full comedy and pathos of the human condition.

We all lead busy lives and sometimes forget to tell our friends how much we love them and how grateful we are for their support throughout the good and bad times in our lives.

These inspiring examples of wit and wisdom, written by real people and based on their true-life experiences, sum up the essence of friendship, and show why our friends will always have a special place in our hearts.

about the author

Anne Howard is an experienced author and editor with several years publishing experience, who specializes in books on families and relationships. From the many hundreds of contributions that were sent to her, she has selected the ones that best sum up what friendship is all about—its joys, its importance, and the qualities that make a good friend.

A friend is there for you when he'd rather be somewhere else.

Life is nothing
without friendship.

Friendship is the source of the greatest pleasures…

…without friends even agreeable pursuits become tedious.

Stay is the most charming word a friend can utter.

Real friends overlook your failures and tolerate your successes.

Friendship improves happiness
and relieves misery, doubles joys,
and divides sorrows.

Friendship is genuine when two people can enjoy each other's company without speaking.

A friend hears the song
in my heart and sings it to me
when my memory fails.

One friend in a
lifetime is much,
two are many,
three are hardly
possible.

A true friend is somebody who can make us do what we can.

A friend is someone you can be alone with and have nothing to do and nothing to say, and be comfortable in the silence.

Friendship is the cement that holds the world together.

A friend asks how you are and waits for the answer.

Without friendship life
has no sweetness.

Growing an old friend takes time.

True friends are a refuge from poverty and other misfortunes.

The best time
to make friends
is before you
need them.

It's easier to make friends
by being interested in
other people than it is by
trying to get people
interested in you.

Friendship gives life and animation to the object it supports.

Friends of the right sort will help to make you happy and successful.

A young man starting out in life needs plenty of friends more than he needs plenty of money.

A good friend is
cheaper than therapy.

A friend is someone who believes
in you and is willing to trust you.

A friend is one of nature's masterpieces.

Friendship is the thread that ties hearts together.

Life is partly what we make it, and partly what it is made by the friends we choose.

I've had many friends with whom I've shared my time, but very few with whom I've shared my heart.

He who has a thousand friends
has not a friend to spare
And he who has one enemy
will meet him everywhere.

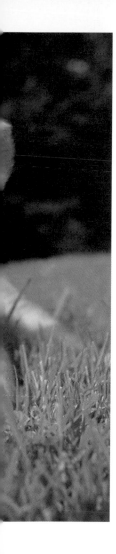

One loyal friend is worth
ten thousand relatives.

A true friend is just, helpful, bold, patient, courageous…

…and unchangeable.

Good friends are angels on earth.

If you see someone without a smile, give them one of yours.

Friends fill your life with joy,
your soul with sunshine, and
your heart with love.

To have a friend, be a friend.

Every man, however wise, needs a friend's advice.

Even a rich man wouldn't want
to live without friends.

True friends listen
to what you
don't say.

Many joys may come
and go but friendship
is forever!

The ornament of a house is the friends who frequent it.

Friends are flowers in the garden of life.

Sometimes a library of words
can't say what a hug from
a friend can.

Robbing life of friendship is like robbing the world of the sun.

A friend is someone who reaches for your hand and touches your heart.

The harmony between friends is sweeter than any choir.

A best friend is like
a four leaf clover,
hard to find and
lucky to have.

Friends, like books, should be few and well chosen.

Blessings come in many ways…

…the nicest come as friends.

A single rose can be my garden…

…a single friend, my world.

Special friends become
our chosen family.

A mirror may reflect a man's face,
but his friends reflect what
he is really like.

Go often to the house
of a friend…

…weeds choke an
unused path.

The worst solitude is to have no real friendships.

Friendship is a gift with strings attached…

…heartstrings!

Your friends know you better in the first minute they meet you than your acquaintances know you in a thousand years.

Every gift from a friend is a wish for your happiness.

Prosperity gives us friends, adversity proves them.

Don't save loving
speeches for your friends
until they are dead.

When I find myself fading,
I close my eyes and realize
my friends are my energy.

It is one of the blessings of old friends that you can afford to be stupid with them.

A friend walks in when
everyone else has walked out.